INTERRUPTED GEOGRAPHIES

Interrupted Geographies

Poems by Iris Jamahl Dunkle

Copyright © Iris Jamahl Dunkle 2017

No part of this book may be used or performed without written consent from the author, if living, except for critical articles or reviews.

Dunkle, Iris Jamahl
1st edition.

ISBN: 978-0-9965864-7-4
Library of Congress Control Number: 2017935373

Interior Layout by Lea C. Deschenes
Cover Design by Dorinda Wegener
Cover Art by Diana Majumdar
Editing by Issa M. Lewis and Tayve Neese

Printed in Tennessee, USA
Trio House Press, Inc.
Ponte Vedra Beach, FL

To contact the author, send an email to tayveneese@gmail.com.

For Andrea, in thanks for the room on the swamp where so much of this was born.

Table of Contents

1. SKY PARLOR

Prayer for Arboglyphs	3
The Waiting	4
Louder than the Sun	5
At Yosemite with Max, Age 6	7
Dear Denise Duhamel—	8
Dear Heart—	10
The Closet	13

2. 500 DAYS

Eridanus Remembers the Flood	17
The Naming of Pithole	18
She Sits Like a Patient upon a Monument and Smiles at Grease	19
The Fire that Burns Continuous	21
In the Days of Mud and Speculation	22
Surface Wells	23
Desire Doesn't Work in Pithole, PA	24
The Grand Ball, July 28, 1865	25
Last Evening Only the Color Gold Could Keep Me	26
The False Front of Want	28

Catherine's Fortune or The Ballad of French Kate	29
Pithole's Purlieu	32
The Pithole Daily Record, September 1865 – 1866	33
Diana: The Dark Voice of Crickets	34
Dead Letters	35
Developing a Moral Climate, Pithole 1865	36
Out	37
Cacoethes	39
The Ballad of Widow Rickets	40
Boom Residue	43
Swear By It	44
What Wears Out or Up After Time	45

3. SPRING AND ALL

How to Cope in a New Landscape	49
Spring Cleaning	50
Housewarming	51
Let Me Introduce You to the Season of Want	52
Tolerance	53
Overnight, Spring Intended Us to Take Her Seriously	54

Storm's Passage	55
[Over the cross, the grave, the skies]	56
The Education of Islands	57
1 Wolf Creek	58
2 Sendai, Japan	59
3 Wolf Creek	60
4 Island	61
The Blue Egg	63
Interrupted Geography	64
Things Given Away	65
Notes	67
Acknowledgments	71

1. SKY PARLOR

*"So, however far you have travelled, your
steps make more holes and the mesh is multiplied—
... exiles must make their own maps."*

—Derek Walcott, *Midsummer*

Prayer for Arboglyphs

The trail rises from the valley—vein to
sky—sometimes granite bedded, sometimes hushed
by pine needles. When we walk it, we walk
for hours. We try to remember each
turn, each nook. Try to find the unmarked way.
Blue skies bury us in expectations.

The creek that threads us up waxes and wanes
between full bellied summer and the ice
of holding its breath. There are days when we
walk through the pygmy pines, wind whispering
like the waves of a lost sea. We giggle
like dryads. Other days the jagged maws
of granite islands swallow us whole
until we can no longer find each other, our way.
Echoes that bend our voices apart.

We aren't the first to want to annotate
this passage of wilderness, no matter how
steep it has become. Half way up, black scar
of an Arboglyph screams from the curved belly
of an aspen tree that we aren't first, or alone.
God bless the tree that remembers the wound of another's experience.

So that when we return to the level
valley floor we hold that carved wilderness
in us—static whisper of aspen leaves,
the course we found, the hope like a hawk's scream
that pierced us until we carried on.

The Waiting

for Jackson

Once you arrived we walked the block like convicts:
you, a tiny bundle in a green felt snowsuit,
me, wearing a body too large to recognize as my own.

The leaves chattered their teeth, the wind shoved us along.
We hadn't found words yet. We spoke in touch.

I point out the monuments of our walk:
Snow White and the Seven Dwarves figurines
tucked behind an abandoned house.
Winter apple trees clinging to their red, shriveled fruit.
The path out—

But always we'd return to the white shuttered house,
to the unbundling, to the flush of warm air awakening our faces.

And each day became a flag strung up to the next—
words formed in your mind like animals hiding in clouds

and you spoke them to me:
thick stones dropped in an ink-dark pool.

Louder than the Sun

When I wake my beloveds in the morning,
they are heavy and clouded as the sky
but also warm and plush
and fogged with dreams.

> *All night the screech owl called and called*
> *to me from the dark woods.*

As they awaken,
I dress their small bodies:
tuck layer after layer in
against what rises
in the world, and in me.

> *On some days history roars*
> *like the creek swollen by storm.*
> *Others, it whispers in the trees tops*
> *that weave in the wind.*

Underneath the day, we lay a track of music
so that we might not hear the past.

> *The skyscrapers jutting*
> *like crooked teeth.*
> *The shirts opening*
> *like terrible blossoms in the fall.*

On our drive to school,
we open the windows to the cool air.
We turn the radio on loud,
sing *brighter than the sun.*

*Sunlight breaking the tops
of green redwood in golden sieves.*

My beloveds smile
and eat tiny waffles—
swaying to the song.
I want to tell my beloveds to remember
bright things, but also what is dark.

*The empty beds. The empty houses.
Empty hearts. But also
what grows out of the soil of memory.*

I want there to be a map,
like a bright star chart:
to show a path
that might make sense, toward safety.

*Because in this world, because in me—
there is ash and clouds of smoke.*

Instead, we warm ourselves
with ourselves and our song.
Instead, the engine burns
on toward our destination.

At Yosemite with Max, Age 6

"Yohhe'meti (Southern Miwok) or Yos.s.e'meti (Central Miwok) originally referred to the Indian tribe that lived in Yosemite Valley. Yosemite means literally "those who kill"

We watch the golden net of leaves fall, then rise from the tree —suspended against the steep shadows of granite cliffs like golden notes. When he stops I see his eyes gather awe. He will not walk on, is fixed and hungry to watch leaves circle in crisp valley air.

Yesterday, at the Visitors Center, we listened to a recorded child's voice speak a history for the Miwok from a diorama filled with plastic ghosts; then, we sat, in a small redwood *kotcha*, his body close, his questions circling mine, circling the stories we had heard. In this sweet darkness there was the scent of earth between history and what's been forgotten.

The valley is a granite bowl where the past still burns a cold silver thread through impossible stone, under a one-eyed moon. Those born here fought to the death to stay.

This is what we do not say. Golden words like leaves netted in air. Lost, but continually returning.

Dear Denise Duhamel—

What is it that boils kettles of red tail hawks in the blue-ceiling of summer sky? Today, there is an animal presence somewhere at our feet—we sense it before we see it. Bird shit on garbage cans. Must be swallows nesting in the eaves. Then, the children spot a fallen chick: half-molted and desperate. Don't touch it. I warn until they return to the house. Too hot to think. I long for descent into the redwood shade and dappled creek so I tell the kids go watch T.V. and take the trash cans down our long, hot driveway. The cans roll large and loud, popping gravel. At the bottom, shade spills relief. The creek trees rustle with animal movement. How do I know how large their bodies are just by the sound? *Is it fear that tethers us in its wake?*

Days like this I feel like a Russian doll: a body carved inside a body. At 22, my girlfriends and I saw a display of middle-aged Barbies at The Body Shop on 17th Avenue in New York. Their plastic bodies had been altered so that they were thick-waisted and C-section scarred. We laughed on stick legs. We spoke in light, hot breaths about how bold the display. Our hearts were still red hummingbirds flying in our chests. Yesterday, I read that Dodo birds swallowed large stones to help them digest, and laughed at how this makes me think only of their disappearance. Women condemned by the Vikings were also made to swallow stones—so many they sunk into the bogs of Schleswig-Holstein. How some were found centuries later – their skin still intact, their red shocks of hair screaming from behind the museum glass. *Perhaps those were only stones the Barbie contained.*

Today what I fear most—what boils in kettles of birds, what crouches and flees from the lean of trees—is this: when I return the small bald bird will just be gone. That no one will be able to read the text of its departure. That my body in its continual awakenings will never swallow the sense and weight of what it contains, of what it has now, or what it will someday become.

Dear Heart—

1

Big lug of muscle. How you drag me down! Don't you know I come from the sort of town that's named after a standoff? Where a man stood three aching-leg days waiting outside the general store for another man who hid inside? Where everything is too fogged in to see clearly? Where the ocean is too cold to swim?

I don't live in a cul-de-sac, heart. I live in a barn on a hill where I can see for miles into the cathedral of sky. Where rain percusses against the tin roof. Where the creek gathers and gathers until there is a storm. Where the trees ache and murmur in the winds. Where the morning sparrows punctuated the sky's blue dome with ellipses that come from the sea. What does it mean to carry something to this place that is so unnameable?

These days I have thick fingers and heavy, slippery feet.

2

Each doctor who has met with my son picks an edge of the tapestry to pull out and name without seeing the whole.

What we are given are small golden threads gathered and rewoven into unrecognizable shapes.

There is a part of me that wants to mitigate the conflict.
That part of me is you, heart.

There is a part of me that steps up to the man standing knee deep in the mud outside of the general store just to whisper in his ear, *you don't want to be remembered for this.*

There is the part of me who is the man waiting for fate to walk in and throw him against the dry goods, to have his face pressed into the dirt floor until he screams.

Heart, that floor is so close, I can smell it.

And then there is my son. My beautiful, suffering son.

3

On the radio program the parents of children with named mental disorders told their stories to the interviewer as if they were in confession. They were honest. They were on the other side of a dark journey looking back.

There was the young child's palpable rage: how it breathed and feathered the air. Or, how the child ran and ran until he could find a tree that could contain the enormous perch of his fear.

There were the holes punched into plaster walls.

There were the volleys of shouts and screams that seemed to echo out from another deeper well of a body.

There were the locked doors, then, the removal of locks.

There were the people brought in to teach safety and discipline to parents who hadn't slept soundly in years.

There was the locking away of knives and scissors and baseball bats (just in case).

There was the teaching of body holds.

There were the words: police intervention.

There was the moment I looked into their stories and saw my own.

4

But what do we do, heart, without a diagnosis? What if we step back only to see the blur of a face. The energy of a being different from what we know to name. But, one we know through the fog, heart. One we cannot live without. One we only want to recognize again.

5

So I step back, heart. I step back and back and try to see the whole tapestry for what it is. I turn off the radio. I dig up the god-damned history of my town and try to understand more than what we've left to speak for itself and I try to write it all down.

Because a story is never simple, heart, is it? Not one that is stitched in my own blood.

The Closet

for Adrienne Rich and Amy Lowell

Today, I am in the dark. Today I am looking for the luminous tree to burn awake in the dark. Like a bare, pocked sycamore I'd written off for countless winters and springs. I'm waiting to see its leaves blaze crimson. I'm waiting for the heat and power of that beauty to enter me.

The panels that contain me are cedar and pungent. There is no light save the high window in the far corner that is soaped by dust. It's open, though, so that the wind that whispers in carries the breath of lilies, the idea of a garden below.

In here, we speak in shadows. My sisters loom large, throwing their images upon the dark walls while I do my best to decipher boundaries – borrowing dark from dark to find sense, but always still distracted by the muffled voices that trickle in from beneath the locked door.

Some days I think the darkness will swallow us—that we'll drown in its ink. Others, the light of early dawn burns the walls awake enough to illuminate the words that have been scrawled up and down the walls. So that I believe in my sisters. So that I believe in the garden below.

One day the door will open and what is contained here will pour out—black velvet dark, or the amethyst stain of dawn. One day we will live like trees, blazing out into the open air. One day our words will wash over their storied houses and reach the garden below.

2. 500 DAYS

"I went travelling to a wreck of a place. There were three gates standing ajar and a fence that broke off. I was not the wreck of anything else in particular. A place came there and crashed. After that it remained the wreck of a place. Light fell on it."

—Anne Carson, "Short Talk on Where to Travel"

Eridanus Remembers the Flood

Rivers were once named
not for their waters,
but for their muddy banks. *(What held them up.)*

Here, Old Man River
still lulls us away
from what's contained. *(Water, the memory of floods.)*

Under the swift, smooth
surface, we perceive
a definite course— *(Forgetting the unseen.)*

so when we awake,
when we arrive, *(At destination, or greatness.)*

like Phaeton, we can't
fight the current of
our own desire. *(Water pulls harder than the sun.)*

The Naming of Pithole

> *"Three hunters paused to rest on an outcrop of sandstone a short distance up the creek and discovered deep fissures in the earth from which there emanated foul-smelling vapors. The snow had melted around the crevices. Curious, one of the hunters decided to investigate further. After squeezing between the rocks, without ascertaining very much, he sat upon the top and dangled his feet over the side. Suddenly he fainted. The companions quickly revived the inquisitive victim and pronounced the holes an exit of Hell, veritably the "Pit" itself."*

This town carries its history dipped in waters too cold to let the mind remember. When the men reached the source of the naming—the pit hole, the black, yawning mouth at the edge of the creek—it was midnight. There were those who leaned over its side cautiously and then, there were those who jumped into the oily dark, into the reek of gas. Each returned with a different story. The hole was a few feet deep, or, the hole was a spacious cavern. On the other side—there were the men who climbed out of the hole. And then, there were the men who learned to tell the history, to try to find sense in the disparity of the many stories that would name the town.

SHE SITS LIKE A PATIENT UPON A MONUMENT AND SMILES AT GREASE

Two years ago, Cornplanter Township was barren.
There were only a few woodsmen who wove
their thin bodies between trees.
Cabins blinked small in the dusk.
Money existed only in imaginations.
Pithole creek was silent all winter,
but sang muddy loud in the spring,
gnashing jagged, rock teeth. No one
noticed the rainbow sheen reflected
on its cool, smooth surface.

Then, on Holden farm,
the wildcatters dug
a well deep enough
to find dark secrets
that would flow without end.
Word spread fast—
ricocheted across great shale valleys—
Everyday people came:
some on foot,
some on horseback,
some sunk in mud to their knees.
Cabins filled fast. Then, tents
built from surrender
of white sheets. There was
so much smoke.   *Just add a broken barrel for a chimney.*
There were so many holes
where the wind licked raw.   *Stuff the cracks with mud and flesh.*

Dig and dig. Bodies ached.
Foot to shovel. Push into the soft earth.

And when Sin Street
opened its red velvet doors
we fell into the pillow-soft flesh.

> *Chill flows down pit hole creek.*
> *Pipes jut, vapors rise in quiet braids.*

And by spring the creek rose
and sang and gnashed
its sharp rock teeth.
And the dry holes filled with water and shame.

The Fire that Burns Continuous

Plank by muddy plank we cover our tracks
this side of the grey river, history
nods off—slips quietly under the icy flow.

> *Fire that burns off an oil well*
> *is the most beautiful fire.*

It's a wooden town we built upon this borrowed land:
smell of new lumber and fresh paint.
What's under (that rot) seeps between the planks.

> *So much to fuel—red velvet—*
> *white heat of extinction—*
> *You forget the loss.*

Plank by muddy plank we name what we've covered
what it once was: *Erielhonian, Senecca, Cornplanter,*
but memory is the stone in the belly that remains
even as the oil wells run dry.

In the Days of Mud and Speculation

By May of 1865, Pithole, or Pithole city, had come to life—fields
of trees cut down and sliced into sticky lumber.

> *We were all optimists:*
> *sun pouring honey*
> *on green budding trees—*
> *mud drying into traversable ruts—*

The smell of pine resin and mud, lumber stacked
and shoved and nailed into crude buildings.

> *No time to dig into the dark,*
> *thick mud for a cellar.*
> *No time gather the rocks*
> *from the creek's bed*
> *to build a foundation.*

10,000 lonely, thirsty men waiting
for spring to bloom over their darkness.

Surface Wells

No one could understand why the oil appeared suddenly. One day the ground became saturated with oil; then, soon after, riddled with holes from which the oil oozed. People who had dug wells for water would now plunge buckets into the dark wells only to return buckets filled with that same sticky dark. The town was rich, but thirsty. Men, women, even young children could be seen walking the muddy streets with a clattering of tin cups, and tea kettles—any shape that could contain water instead of oil. Oil might buy coffee or tea, but it would not make it.

Desire Doesn't Work in Pithole, PA

Fitting that desire's meaning is derived
from the stars. Under that talcum powder light,
against a dark, tree-scaped sky, love seems
bright, reachable.
                      Here, where towns burn monthly,
where what's left washes out from under our
feet, desire still feels like a distant
constellation.
                But, somewhere in the dark oil that rises
is where this all began: a dark hole that
glistens, thick with oil. What rises to
the surface is the possibility,
the risk,
        of a star gone years before we'd
even begun to wish for it.

The Grand Ball, July 28, 1865

The Astor Hotel, Pithole's first, was built
from green wood and sheer will in a single day.
Now, in the dark night, light pours golden from
the cracks that have opened between the boards.

The night of the first Grand Ball, the dust and the gamblers
who nested on the front steps in makeshift games were swept away.
The Oil men washed and shaved. A few women (brought in
from neighboring towns) were escorted into the glowing hotel.

For one night, the thin boards held elegance:
Women's long beaded gowns caressed rough wood floors,
white linen cloths were stretched over wooden tables,
men smoked in their dark suits, and the air was alive
with soft light, champagne and waltzes.

For one long night, the rest of the town could watch it
from straw beds and makeshift huts, even from the eaves of derricks:

honey glow of wealth seeping out
through the cracks into the dark oil of night.

Last Evening Only the Color Gold Could Keep Me

1

The train moved smooth across the landscape as if the whole universe were covered in black ice. When he greeted me at the station I could smell deceit. It breathed through his skin. We took a wagon up the steep hill to the town, if you could call it that. A muddy hill sheathed in newly rutted streets. We got out at a place on First, not a hotel as I'd been told, but a brothel. I could smell the sweat and sin. It oozed into the dark mud. When I screamed he grabbed my arm, looked me in the eye and said, *you'll either fuck the men I bring to you, or starve.*

2

When he threw me in, the attic was lit with the gold lace of sun shining through the beams. *Only the gold can keep me* I thought, my mind swelling with hunger behind the locked door.

3

At first light, the room illumes: a dusty box of hats, a dirty mattress curled into the corner, a few sheets of crumbled paper, a pen.

And so I began the letter to my mother. *It was a lie. Please save me. I am locked in an attic on First Street in Pithole, PA.*

I fold it carefully, slip it between the slats of the wooden room that contains me, and watch it flutter down to the dark, dark mud of the street below.

4

There are so many swollen days. My body gone black and blue with beatings. My mind tethered from my body. A star that blinks from far off.

How the letter was found and mailed is beyond me. But one afternoon I woke still blurred in sleep and muted by hunger to hear a thunder of men in the downstairs. I was carved in golden light—like each piece of me would break off into tiny wings, when the door was kicked in.

My mother walked in, tear-streaked. She gathered me up.

The False Front of Want

There was never enough for us to eat
in this town. The false-fronted hotels
lured the newly rich with ideas of wealth:
a bright red lobster shipped by train, wagon,
a week's journey from the coast to its death,
but never any fruits or vegetables.
Most stood in long lines in front of *Wiggins
Restaurant*. We'd stand on the porch, in lines
that wrapped the dusty block, waiting for the
hollow ring of the dinner bell. Quarter
bought a sandwich, dollar bought a full plate:
meat and potatoes sopped with gravy. If,
by chance, a barrel of oranges found
its way in, you'd read about it in the paper.

Catherine's Fortune
or The Ballad of French Kate

This is my house. Just under a fortnight ago we were getting low on staff. Girls get tired of the business after a few months and figure out how to run off.

Ben came up with the idea: an ad in the Buffalo paper advertising our "hotel", how we need young girls to join our staff. I got a real belly laugh when I read it. Didn't expect much, but then half a dozen girls rolled in from New York. Most are young and inexperienced and real surprised when they walk through the door. It don't take long to turn them around.

A day or more locked up. A good fuck or two by Ben. Threats that we are gonna find and kill their families and they open their legs.

When this last girl got off the train she was green as a sapling. I knew right away she'd be hard to break. But, I got my ways. So does Ben. It's been 10 days and she's still holding out.

Tomorrow, I'll tell Ben scare the fuck into her. If we let her go much longer, she's gonna be too weak to fuck anyone for weeks.

I wasn't always a Madame. I used to live in an elegant house away from dust and mud.

I wore the finest gowns and was waited on by a full staff. My husband, Confederate General LeConte, was well respected in New Orleans. He adored me every day he was alive. Damn that war. What was I supposed to do? Live off that measly pension? Graciously accept the note: Thank you ma'am. Your husband was a fine citizen. I don't give a damn about this country. I had myself a fine life until it was taken. What was I to do? Learn a trade?

I've always been good with men. Since I was a little girl, I could charm all my father's friends. The boys at school would follow me like a pack of starving dogs.

Turning tricks came naturally to me. I liked the power I held over men. Touch the right place and they'd look at you like you were a god.

I started pulling tricks in New Orleans, but my old reputation got in the way of who I wanted to become so I headed East. I met Ben in New York. He was with a traveling gymnastics show as the strong man. He came to the house where I worked looking for a good fuck. I'll never forget the first time he saw me naked before him. Right then, I knew I had him under my thumb.

Within a few months we had both settled in Pithole and set up shop. It was Ben's idea. "It'll be a racket!" He said with a big, dumb grin.

"Ain't enough women to fuck in that town." He became my business partner. I'm tough and have no problem keeping those girls in line but when it comes to angry johns it helps to have Ben's six-and-a-half-feet looming next to me.

This town is a fountain of money. Those boys hit oil, get cash, and give it right back to me. They drink it away at my bar, they fuck it away with my girls and I just smile and open my palm.

Once, a few years ago, I got a letter from my old life: Mrs. LeMurre, a neighbor and friend in New Orleans. Her husband was also a confederate general, so we were close during the war. But, when the war ended and her husband came home, and mine did not, I couldn't stand her. What's worse is she never even knocked on my door to offer her condolences. She'd just peek through her curtains every once in a while, to watch my decline: first, the furniture taken away, then servants being let go. Then, finally, the men I began to let in as I learned my new trade. I'll give her this, she never called the cops on me. She just kept those curtains closed tight once she knew what was going on.

That's why I never opened her letter. Those first few months came rushing back to me in a terrible wave. I nearly drowned. So, I threw her letter down in the muddy street. It was undoubtedly a letter of regret where she pours out her heart— how she'd wished she been there to help me in my time of need.

How, if only she had, my life wouldn't have taken this terrible turn.

How she hopes now she can become my friend again and save me.

Well, Mrs. LeMurre, my fortune ain't as bad as you make it out. I got more power in Pithole than you'd ever wish for. My girls are the best in town because I train them that way.

They know how to make men beg for more. I don't need your god damned pity.

How do you like being face down in the mud?

Pithole's Purlieu

In this purlieu, one ranged at large. No law
or confines—Pithole still young, still a live
hive of bodies, without center, a swarm
of destructive tides. Waiting for a decree
to declare it a real town. Until then,
we were left to handle it on our own:
shit, water, law. A lone justice of peace,
a pair of sheriffs trying to tether
the wild streets down. We watched our future
fly, far off, like a string-less kite until
it had drifted too far to see. After,
those who would return to the deep grass field
that was once our town, came heads down
leaving stones—a foundation of regret—behind.

The Pithole Daily Record, September 1865 – 1866

Charles C. Wicker came to Pithole with just a bag of type, some ink and a dream of setting up a small print shop. A few weeks later, he'd leased a room and the first issue of the town's new public conscience, *The Pithole Daily Record*, hit muddy streets and stuck. Amongst advertisements, and national news, the raspy voice of Pithole shone through: the dead and dying, the babies born, even a long list of unclaimed mail. Every loose end was documented in hard copy. Crocus, who would become Pithole's key correspondent, eloquently merged fact and fiction: the way oil met mud, the way everything merged in Pithole.

Diana: The Dark Voice of Crickets

I can see the whole dusty street
from my seat in front of the Syracuse Hotel.
Young men walk by still blackened by oil and dust.
Can't imagine what it's like to sleep in the eaves
of the derricks. Over the constant rhythm
of oils' give and take. Bet they dream of lobster and champagne.

After they pass me, too tired to catcall,
they line up for a good meal at *Wiggins*.
I feel real lucky for the straw bed I've got.
Not to mention the solid walls, minus a gap or two,
where eyes peek through while I lay with a customer.
Months ago, I would have blushed.
But, now, when I lay down, the world goes cold
and slack as a winter sky. He don't look me in the eye.
Why open my mind? Those are my constellations.

At night, when I'm finally alone on my straw bed,
I close my eyes and listen to the sound of crickets.
Pretend their dark voices weave my song of escape
back to the pine woods and the sound of the sea breathing.
I can still see my husband's face looming over me
soft and comforting as a moon, before his dead face
eclipses my memory. Turns home unrecognizable.

Dead Letters

Weather bore down hard on the snaking line:
100s of men and women wrap the dusty
façade of Pithole's new Post Office.

Clever newsboys who got up at dawn
got spots, and then sold off them off for $10.
Letters increased each week until Pithole's
Post was the third busiest in the state.
All day, a live wire of bodies pulsed
in and out the door, sending stacks of cash,

scatterings of words home, then waiting
for a voice to echo back. But many

letters were left unclaimed. Each week, the newspaper
printed the names of the unclaimed letters: *Dear Louise, why*

don't you write back? Letters piling like snow
foretelling the coming winter. While just

a few doors down from these words the girls stare
out from the thin, slated walls of brothels.

Developing a Moral Climate, Pithole 1865

The newly erected Methodist Church
perched white and steepled on the hill's steep crest.
Pithole now had dozens of children running
in its muddy streets, but when the Reverend
Steadfast stood at the pulpit, asked,

> *what is a man profited if he gain the whole world and lose his own soul?*
> *This town needs a foundation; our children need a school.*

the collection plate came back light. So,
being a man of action, he opened the church doors
and took to the streets. As everyone in Pithole knew,
liquor was sold illegally in each velvet curtained hotel.
The Reverend Steadfast turned them in,
then used the collected fines to set up the school
in the belly of the stone church.

Years later, when the wooden boom town would
burn, all that remained was that church basement
where the children had finally gotten to learn.

Out

*"Thus in nine months the wilderness had become
metropolis, with railroads, plank roads and pipelines."*

For months the Teamsters
ruled the oil trade in Pithole—

*each barrel bled from the earth
had to be carried out.*

$3.25 a barrel to hire a man
to carry the load down
to the Oil City Depot—

*High atop the hills, Pithole
was never meant to be a city.*

Against this monopoly,
wood plank roads were built—

*Like teeth sunk
into the muddy hillside.*

Then, two railroads battled
to gain the business
of ground transport:

*one followed the lip of the Allegheny river,
then wound up Pithole creek.
The other climbed steep
as a rollercoaster
over the hills between.*

Then, with much success
the 3-inch pipes were laid down—

>> *Metal arteries draining*
the hill of its blood.

The Teamsters screamed
from the burning mouth
of the barn they occupied.
"It will be the end of this town!"

>> *The smoke rolling out over their heads.*

When others tried to stop them,
tried to wet the roofs
of neighboring buildings,
the Teamsters flamed
the blossom of fire
and shot their guns into the air.

>> *Not long after, the Teamsters would leave.*
Not long after, the town would burn.

Cacoethes

No water for weeks and we became mad
with desire. Fires grew more numerous.

> *Green wood burns fast and hot.*

We stitched Hook and Ladder together, but

there was no water. You can only watch so much burn
before your throat and heart burn too.

> *Sun pouring through buildings like sieves.*

First, we watched the burning barrels of oil

multiply—lit smooth with velvet fire.
We were *hypnotized by the lick of flames.*

Then, Brown Street—glass shattering outward like shouts
from each hotel's red carpeted throats.

> *Women, half-naked, streaming out into muddy streets.*

When soot-black horses galloped out
of the Chautauqua Livery Stable

their manes aflame,
> *Comets spelling out into oily dark night.*

we knew not to follow, not to try to read
the text of their bright, shimmering paths.

The Ballad of Widow Rickets

1

I remember the way the water would
reflect the clouds as I'd pull the bucket
up from the well. Ten hours a day, bent,
washing the mud from each lost heart's shirt.
Then, after I'd finish, how good it felt to
sit back in the cool shade beneath the last
hemlock (*not yet cut for lumber*). Mine was
a simple life. Not rich, but good enough.
There's always washing to be taken in.
The hotel linens, the shirts of weary
or elated boys, the girls who can't look
you in the eye. Down on luck, or striking
it rich, there is always mud and dirt and
oil. There is always something to wash.

2

That night, I heard the screams first.
Then, the sound of glass bursting, hot rush
of air. I ran out into the dark,
found the Syracuse hotel engulfed in flame.
Just far enough away, a mob gathered
in their own fear: 30 or 40 women and men,
half-clothed, mud and soot-streaked.
When they saw me they came back to life,
running past me to my well—like I brought
the thought of water to them. In minutes,
we'd formed a fire line—passing buckets,
dousing the fire's hunger, body to body, hand to hand.

3

By dawn, we were up to our knees in mud
and ash. The hotel smoldering, but the
surrounding houses spared. We unstitched our
weary bodies from the line that had held
us up. I took a few girls home with me
(they didn't have anywhere to go). Set
them up with a few blankets and chairs in
the pallor before I crumpled into
my own bed. It wasn't until noon when
I awoke with a tremendous thirst. Light
peered in, and my face was flushed with its heat.
So, I took a bucket to the well. What
rose to the surface was dark and sticky
as the night we'd survived. *Oil* I screamed,
until the girls came and thirst closed my throat.

4

The well was dry of water, but oil
flowed steadily for 9 weeks straight. The girls
I'd brought home from the fire now helped me
retrieve the oil. We filled every
wash basin full. Dirty clothes piled in
untouched mounds all over the house. By noon,
the men had gotten word. They brought barrels,
and offers to take charge of operations.
By the second day, seven had proposed.
We just laughed, took the barrels, and kept on.
The men started digging up every
other well in town with no luck. Then, one
day, the oil just stopped. I dropped the bucket
down and found only clear, blue sky and clouds
 reflecting back up at me from the dark.

5

It didn't take much to pack up shop. We
hitched a wagon, tied on our belongings
and waved goodbye to this oil-sick town.
The men were still optimistic. They trailed
the wagon on foot offering last chance
proposals. We just urged the horses on.
Leaving them to their dusty hope and thirst.
At the train station, I handed each girl
a ticket home, and a bit of money.
We were a sight! Hugging each other on
the platform, our lives untying. I looked out
of the train window the whole ride home. Watched
the river wander away from the sharp
shale cliffs, clouds carried on its brown surface.

Boom Residue

When the ground is stripped of all living things—
what remains? A few jagged trees that jut
like exclamation points from the impasse
of the knee-deep muck of mud and oil.

> *In arithmetic, the remainder (or*
> *residue) is the amount "left over".*

Derricks, built of green wood, and wooden hope,
by now, stud the valley and in their eaves
sleep the young men (some still in their teens, still
raw from war). They lease dreams by sixteenths.

> *One in eight wells yielded oil. One in*
> *twelve gave oil in paying quantities.*

Under cadence of engines their fiery dreams
burn off to reveal fortune or escape.

Swear By It

Swear by this shallow sand town—this wish cloud—
this poor farmland dug up, deforested
and carved into muddy streets and leased lots.
Swear by the farmers who sold off little
and stayed on in their tiny log cabins
at the quick-built luxury of velvet
carpeted hotels, who swerve through drunken,
rutted streets on sleds carried by oxen.
Swear you will not thirst. Swear the shadow that
carried you—that plucked you from your small town
with the lure of OIL! RICHES! will not
cover you like a shroud. When the town burns
(and it will burn) don't run. Instead, look for
the quiet lamp, far off, steady on the
Copeland Farm. Know that star, walk to its stubborn,
steady light until the greed burns off.
Until you are safe.

What Wears Out or Up After Time

Out of the valley mist that low hollow hangs.
Out of the moan of thick river ice pull gone locked.
Come melt. Come rainbow sheen, glistening.
Come wool of clouds opening up.

Out of the forest thins. Down hemlock,
split pine. Up the derrick still sap-sticky.
Up the open-bellied stores and hotels.
Up the facade and the see-through-the-cracks.
Come the war-tired boys still blind of love,
still hungry, still pistol-armed.

Out of thirst and holes and mud comes oil.
Red velvet curtains gone muddy,
creek gone muddy loud,
comes screams of hairless horses,
their burning bodies spelling into night.
Out of the locked up girls who open their legs because of fists.

Come something red as cardinals. Out of bread lines and dead letters
and lost children come thick pipes and steel laid down to out.
Come spit in your face. Come hot breath.

Come the fold in, the knock down, the every man for himself,
the bury it, the get out, the fire that burns to the ground.

Come the ashes sifting down. Come the years.
The heavy dirt that don't rise 'til you dig in.
Come the buried river, still moving.
Come the ghosts of those girls, thick hair blossoming—
Come the words still whispered from their lips.

3. SPRING AND ALL

> *"But now the stark dignity of entrance–Still, the profound change has come upon them: rooted, they grip down and begin to awaken"*

—William Carlos Williams, *Spring and All*

How to Cope in a New Landscape

First, learn the promise of water. Listen
to the wind, believe what it will carry.

Get a shovel, dig. Under every
town there is a secret room no talks about.

Sometimes, this room is spotless. But sometimes,
it contains a small, forgotten child.

Work tirelessly to retrieve the child
even if no one will confirm that she exists.

Second, learn to forget the press of fog,
the sharp taste of salt in the air. Forget

the landscape you've stitched into your skin. Wash
yourself in the new air—no matter how cold.

Third, step off of the crumbling asphalt
onto the spongy earth. Find acceptance

in what will rebuild each Spring. No matter where
you end up, there will be birds, some unknown.

Identify them. Follow their jagged
ascent. Identify trees and common

plants and animals. Don't infer meaning
from names alone. Look deep into the woods

until you see what was unseen. Soon a
song will rise in your throat.

Spring Cleaning

Last night, warm wind baptized the still damp earth.
By dawn, the birds were quieted by dizzying nets of snow.
Spring and all its myths comes slow and muzzled here.
No pomegranate-stained fingers yet touch the sky.

Only a lone yellow crocus nuzzles
up from the dead, grey leaves. Fearless, or blind
to which season Kore turns her cheek.

Housewarming

The day we arrived the birdfeeder swung violently empty. The swamps yawned with ice. The sky frowned grey and hurried upon us.

The day we arrived the wind whispered small prayers or curses. The grass was lost beneath crust of snow. The geese departed in careful choreography, their voices echoing against the sky.

The day we arrived we rubbed our minds raw with sandpaper, afraid our belief would shine through. We bound our arms and legs in scraps of worry and shame, dreaming of winter melt and blue skies.

But no matter how careful we were, no matter how bound, in the night, the starlight and the moonlight crept on tiny white feet into our room gathering our whispers. And every morning we would awaken to our own gossamer truths strung along the tops of the hemlock trees, jeweled with dew. We would awaken to a dawn chorus—a shock of red cardinals in the white doubt of snow—singing the truths we could never forget.

Let Me Introduce You to the Season of Want

Rain falls with insidious intent to tell *to tell to tell*. Shale cliffs shed their secrets once covered in ice, chip by jagged chip. *How to reverse this erasure?*

How to find words buried deep in our throats—words that glowed red as coals—those long winter nights. Soon, Spring will erupt flower-hungry. New rain will wash (no, bare) what was covered. Let me introduce you to the thin, white roots of history no longer under the influence of winter stupor and ice.

We are digging now.
We are covered in our filth.

Tolerance

Today, half-a-dozen blue herons rose in awkward strokes
from their nests in the tall, bare trees. Logic suggests

they are rising for hunger. Not that they are
rising toward God or the perfect blue camouflage of skies.

In this town sewn shut by the coarse threads
of *belief* even the birds will not rise.
Those herons are a lie. So are the skies.

Under the grey press of another cold dawn,
help me learn how to untie what binds
the birds' large muscular bodies to the tree.
Help me stop what carries from tongue to swollen tongue.

Overnight, Spring Intended Us to Take Her Seriously

The machine whir of frog swell
rises from the swamp, lulling

us through the open mouths of windows
into sleep. But, by dawn's stain, earth had offered

too much growth for us to bear overnight—

> Dangling, heavy-nosed daffodils
> cover soggy green fields with
> their awkward yellow bodies.
> Skunk cabbage opens the swamp
> to the broad questions
> of their deep, green leaves.

Everywhere—fecund scents rise belligerently to meet us—
to break the silence of white fields.

Where I'm from, Spring rose politely—scent of rosemary,
after first rain, low fog whispers time is never lost.

O forget, O walk into the warm swell of air against sleeping skin.

Storm's Passage

Impossible not to hear the stuttering
rain on glass panes, the whispers of traffic miles off,
the punctuated moan of the far off train.

Impossible not to swallow this passage—
or want of it, like dark bread broken in the night
and shared with the lost.

Impossible not to gather the miles like wet leaves—

Headlights swelling past
on this grid of desire.

[Over the cross, the grave, the skies]

On Wolf Creek, the water ebbs and flows. Come
spring a new path is forged from flood of snow
melt, overpowering the boundaries.
Until fall when the water will sink back
into itself, toward stasis, speaking
only in cold whispers that spill from cracks
in the ice like breath. *All are saved whether
they know it or not.* Then, the nameless voice:
green, fecund screams, thrust and ache from its banks.
Uncurling lips of skunk grass, steady-eyed
gaze of the white iris. Still, the voice of
reason will swim in the deep of the creek—
a forgotten, shadowy trout. Look hard,
long enough, you might catch a silver glint.

The Education of Islands

"O for God's sake
they are connected
underneath

They look at each other
across the glittering sea
some keep a low profile

Some are cliffs
The Bathers think
islands are separate like them"

—Muriel Rukeyser, "Islands" from *The Gates*

1 Wolf Creek

Sunday, I enter the stone church,
mind cavernous as the space,
trying to unfold the origami of my thoughts—
must be a shedding of logic to find,
in this hollow space, a center.

> *There is no ocean here. No tang of salt in air.*
> *Wolf Creek whispers beneath crack of ice.*

The wooden pews are filled, on each lap
a bible open to the passage read by the Pastor.

> *God revealed in the cracks between words.*

2 SENDAI, JAPAN

Standing at the edge of Matsushima Bay so many years ago,
I was the other—   *to myself, to my host family.*

Awkwardness of my teenage body and mind
slipping from my fingers—
                    dozo yoroshiku—nice to meet you.

Today, the news informed us
the wave that hit Sendai, Japan
was all consuming—
before photographs,
before voices of those who survive,
my memories float up,
weightless as paper ashes,
rising in the remaining heat:

> *Feeling of humid air on my teenage skin.*
> *Taste of rice balled, and at its center a sweetness.*
> *Scent of oak planks, earth aching beneath the ancient temple.*
> *An archipelago—islands spelling safe passage toward self.*

3 Wolf Creek

A few days after the Tsunami,
I return to the stone, inland church
trying to construct sense from loss—

> *miles wind round and round my wrists.*

Here, the God revealed is constructed of fear, not love.

> *I have not yet heard if the islands survived.*
> *I have not yet heard if the people who cared for me survived.*

The faces looking at me—   *or through me*
appear at times to be made of cardboard.
This week, in Bible study class, we discuss the Tsunami.
"Is God angry because many Japanese aren't Christian?"
"Is this disaster what they deserve, since they live on a fault line?"

> *Not, here is where you can send blankets and food*
> *Not, gather the bright red strings of your compassion.*

Hate flickers and licks the air around us.
What grows between us isn't an island   *It is the emptiness*
                        before the island was born of the earth.

4 Island

> *What happens when the place*
> *of memory no longer exists?*
> *If language is also a map of failures,*
> *what is the muscular residue*
> *that burns and spits*
> *between words?*

Between these words I carry my grief.

> *Volcanic eruptions*
> *calmed into form by sea water*

Mapping a path, constructing a language of air and ash. Even here.

Because I believe in the islands, *rough rock,*
populated by gnarled and weathered pine trees

I dig into the deep, blue waters,
look for the islands I have not yet seen.

> *The heart of the person before you is a mirror.*

When I open my mouth
the words that soar out
are constructed of rock.

"There is a place in Japan called Matsushima:
a deep blue sea filled with thousands of islands."

Around the table
the parishioners listen: *their imaginations spit and spark.*

"The people who live there are like you."

There are ladders underneath, no matter how deep.

The Blue Egg

This morning, a great blue heron rose from the swamp like the second coming. I'd never seen the high nests in the far-off trees until he rose. Green buds are pulsing out of the fingers of trees and the long sleep is shaken from our bodies as we stumble back into the spotty light. All winter in our borrowed home my son has been collecting egg cartons. Every week he stores another cardboard carton beneath the sink. *"For the chickens, Momma."* He says. *"When we raise chickens, we can sell the eggs."* The sky sits above the trees—blue as the heron. Blue as a dyed egg. Blue as a promise. When the bird rose this morning he brought what was land bound (our hearts, our eyes) up to the possibility of sky.

Interrupted Geography

Each day shifts its weight against plates of time.
New month opens like the mouth of a dip-slip:
fissures from which we arise still blinking
and haunted by the past. *What got me here?*

Did chance land me in this other landscape?
And if so, how do I tell it? I don't
know the species of trees or birds. Stories
that whisper from the grey river just come
apart in my hands when I kneel at its
muddy banks, trying to gather them up.

Still, I can't lose the education of
earthquakes. What's under me now may *(no, will)*
rise up, so best to get to know it.

Things Given Away

A sharp tongue, clear mind,
sound of hawks circling; life
strung between two pines,

instruction of flight;
salty promise of fog; first
garden of kale and

red onions nuzzled
by deer; dirt road, the dusty
wash toward impasse; sound

of the far off creek
howling after a hard rain;
A quieted tongue;

a place that washes
away with each passing rain.

Notes

"Sky Parlor" is the name Amy Lowell gave to her bedroom on the top floor of Sevenels, her family home where she later lived as an adult with her partner, Ada Dwyer Russell. The house was known for its incredible gardens. When Amy Lowell died suddenly in 1925 and left the house to Russell, the Lowell family wouldn't grant her final wishes. They sold the property and the sky parlor and all of the gardens were removed.

"At Yosemite with Max, Age 6": The note at the beginning of the poem is from the definition for "Yosemite" found in the glossary of *Myths of the Southern Sierra Miwok* by S.A. Barrett. Also, "kotcha" is the name of the traditional redwood dwellings of the Miwok.

"Prayer for Arboglyphs": arboglyphs are tree carvings made in the bark of aspen trees by shepherds, many of them Basque and Irish American, throughout the Western United States.

"500 Days": The city of Pithole in western Pennsylvania looks today much as it looked in December 1865, just before oil was found and the barley fields of Thomas Holden's farm were dug up to become muddy streets paved in blood and desire. It is a huge empty field, spotted with a few trees rolling down in a steep slope to Pit Hole Creek. The Holden brothers knew little about the oil boom that was taking place in nearby Titusville. In fact, in the Pithole area, little money was used or circulated; rather, farms were self-sustaining and what was needed that couldn't be produced was bartered for. Then, two men: Frazier and Faulkner wandered up from their successful oil wells in Titusville to the farm located on Pithole creek in order to do a bit of wildcatting. In January 1865, they dug the United States Well, or Frazier well, which would fast become the highest producing well in US history—producing upwards of 250 barrels of oil per day in the first two weeks. What ensued was mayhem. Word got out through newspapers across the nation and within a four month period Pithole grew out of the Holden fields. From its onset, Pithole was doomed to fail. It was a boom town—a town built on excitement and greed. Prather, who bought the town off Frazier and Faulkner didn't sell lots; instead, he leased them out. So, no one who came to Pithole came to stay. They came to borrow land, and either strike it rich on oil, or strike it rich off of those who were striking it rich off oil. And boy did people come. Men poured into town to find their fortunes. Buildings were erected overnight without foundations from the green lumber of nearby trees. No house had a basement. And as the sun started to pour down in the late spring, people said you could see through the houses like sieves. Women and young girls (some as young as eleven) were lured to town and forced into sexual slavery. As you can imagine, a town like this didn't last long. In fact, legend has it that the town lasted only 500 days. But, during that brief period the extreme wealth that poured through the town (at its peak nearly $1,000, 000 per day) created a plethora of stories still being gathered from the mud and ashes that would remain.

"Eridanus Remembers the Flood": Eridanus refers to a river found in Greek mythology.

"The Naming of Pithole": The quotation that begins the poem is from *Pithole: the Vanished City* by William Culp Darrah (1).

"She Sits Like a Patient upon a Monument and Smiles at Grease": The title of this poem is from a book about the history of Pithole written by Crocus, Pithole's famed newspaper man.

"The Fire that Burns Continuous": The names listed in this poem—*Erielhonian, Senecca, Cornplanter*—are there in remembrance. The early Native American tribe Erielhonian were taken over by the Senecca tribe (led by the Native American Diplomat, Cornplanter).

"Out": The quotation at the beginning of the poem is from *Pithole: The Vanished City* (115).

"[Over the cross, the grave, the skies]": The title of this poem is taken from the hymn "Christ the Lord has Risen Today" by Charles Wesley.

Acknowledgments

"The Waiting" *Poetry City* USA Fall 2016

"Prayer for Arboglyphs" *Chicago Quarterly Review* Spring 2016

"The Closet" *Adrienne Rich: a Tribute Anthology* 2012

"Dear Heart—" *Inside Out: Literature of Mental Illness* 2015

"Dear Denise Duhamel—" *Talking Writing* 2013

"How to Cope in a New Landscape" Knightville Poetry Contest Finalist, *The New Guard* 2011

"Housewarming" *Ginger Piglet* Fall 2012

"The Blue Egg" *The Prose Poem Project* December 2012

"Let Me Introduce You to the Season of Want" *Coal Hill Review* Spring 2015

"What Wears Up or Out After Time" and "Swear by It" *Lake Effect* 2015

"The Fire that Burns Continuous" and "Cacoethes" *Volt* issue 17, 2012

"[Over the Cross, the Grave, the Skies]" *Sugar Mule* , Issue 48, 2015

About the Author

Iris Jamahl Dunkle is the current Poet Laureate of Sonoma County, CA. Her second poetry book, *There's a Ghost in this Machine of Air*, is about the untold history of Sonoma County, CA, and was published in November 2015 by Word Tech Editions. Her debut poetry collection, *Gold Passage*, was selected by Ross Gay to win the 2012 Trio Award, and was published by Trio House Press in 2013. Her chapbooks, *Inheritance* and *The Flying Trolley*, were published by Finishing Line Press in 2010 and 2013. Her poetry, essays and creative non-fiction have been published widely in numerous publications including *Fence, Calyx, Catamaran, Poet's Market 2013, JMWW*, and *Chicago Quarterly Review*. Of note, her poem, "How to Cope in a New Landscape," was a finalist for the The New Guard's Knightville Poetry Contest, and her poem "The Trick of Sound" was a finalist for the *Yalobusha Review*'s Yellowwood Poetry Prize. Her essay, "Yellow Dahlias," was nominated for a Pushcart prize. She is currently writing a biography on Charmian Kittredge London. Dunkle teaches writing and literature at Napa Valley College. She received her B.A. from the George Washington University, her M.F.A. in Poetry from New York University, and her Ph.D. in American Literature from Case Western Reserve University. She is on the staff of the Napa Valley Writers conference, and currently resides with her family in Northern California.

About the Artist

Since a very early age **Diana Majumdar** has been exposed to art in many forms and shapes. Growing up in Estonia in the last days of the Soviet Union she was first introduced to art through her father. He taught her the basics of watercolor, took her to see the museums of Estonia, Russia, Armenia, and gave her his large set of art books printed in Russian and Armenian. So when the choice for a field of studies presented itself after Diana came to California, the choice was easy. She graduated from the Academy of Art University in San Francisco last Spring with the Fine Art degree. The Academy offered the opportunity to explore different subject matter from traditional landscape paintings and still-life to portraiture. Experimenting with different media was a major part of the experience at the Academy. Her work reflects this variety of exposure, using mediums such as watercolor and oils or charcoal and pastels in a piece of work. Combination provides opportunities for experimentation and unlimited possibilities. Most recent body of work is inspired by nature and features encaustic as one more element. Diana loves the ability to create a veiled, dreamy look. Wax allows for layers to recede or even hide. This medium doesn't let her become too precise or realistic. "I just have to let it flow and let it happen", she says. Layering, obscuring and revealing are integral components of her works. You can see more of her paintings at:

http://www.dianamajumdarart.com/

About the Book

Interrupted Geography was designed at Trio House Press through the collaboration of:

Issa M. Lewis, Lead Editor
Tayve Neese, Supporting Editor
Diana Majumdar, Cover Art
Dorinda Wegener, Cover Design
Lea Deschenes, Interior Design

The text is set in Adobe Caslon Pro.

The publication of this book is made possible, whole or in part, by the generous support of the following individuals and/or agencies:

Anonymous

About the Press

Trio House Press is a collective press. Individuals within our organization come together and are motivated by the primary shared goal of publishing distinct American voices in poetry. All THP published poets must agree to serve as Collective Members of the Trio House Press for twenty-four months after publication in order to assist with the press and bring more Trio books into print. Award winners and published poets must serve on one of four committees: Production and Design, Distribution and Sales, Educational Development, or Fundraising and Marketing. Our Collective Members reside in cities from New York to San Francisco.

Trio House Press adheres to and supports all ethical standards and guidelines outlined by the CLMP.

Trio House Press, Inc. is dedicated to the promotion of poetry as literary art, which enhances the human experience and its culture. We contribute in an innovative and distinct way to American Poetry by publishing emerging and established poets, providing educational materials, and fostering the artistic process of writing poetry. For further information, or to consider making a donation to Trio House Press, please visit us online at: www.triohousepress.org.

Other Trio House Press Books you might enjoy:

Bird~Brain by Matt Mauch, 2017

The Short Drive Home by Joe Osterhaus
    2016 Louise Bogan Award Winner selected
    by Chard deNiord

Dark Tussock Moth by Mary Cisper
    2016 Trio Award Winner selected
    by Bhisham Bherwani

Break the Habit by Tara Betts, 2016

Bone Music by Stephen Cramer
    2015 Louise Bogan Award selected by Kimiko Hahn

*Rigging a Chevy into a Time Machine and Other Ways
    to Escape a Plague* by Carolyn Hembree
    2015 Trio Award Winner selected by Neil Shepard

Magpies in the Valley of Oleanders by Kyle McCord, 2015

Your Immaculate Heart by Annmarie O'Connell, 2015

The Alchemy of My Mortal Form by Sandy Longhorn
    2014 Louise Bogan Winner selected by Carol Frost

What the Night Numbered by Bradford Tice
    2014 Trio Award Winner selected by Peter Campion

Flight of August by Lawrence Eby
    2013 Louise Bogan Winner selected by Joan Houlihan

The Consolations by John W. Evans
    2013 Trio Award Winner selected by Mihaela Moscaliuc

Fellow Odd Fellow by Steven Riel, 2013

Clay by David Groff
    2012 Louise Bogan Winner selected by Michael Waters

Gold Passage by Iris Jamahl Dunkle
    2012 Trio Award Winner selected by Ross Gay

If You're Lucky Is a Theory of Mine by Matt Mauch, 2012

www.ingramcontent.com/pod-product-compliance
Lightning Source LLC
Chambersburg PA
CBHW020622300426
44113CB00007B/745